IF IT AIN'T ONE THING TO GROW THROUGH IT'S ANOTHER:

INTERACTIVE HEALING BOOK OF QUOTES AND SHORT STORIES

A Mother's Guide To Healing And Building A Better Future

1st
EDITION

Mirror Management

www.daijahb.com

Thank you for your investment in becoming a better version of yourself. I am so grateful that my mother, grandmothers, aunties, cousins, counselors, mentors, and more chose to invest time into me along this journey called motherhood and even before. I hope that what they've instilled in me will spark something in you, and you take something from this workbook to start you on your journey to creating a finger licking LOAF of bread that sticks together no matter how many knives come to slice you based on the ingredients of (love.opportunity.awareness.forgiveness) #loaf #mirrormanagement #asilearnyoulearn #l.o.a.f

TABLE OF CONTENTS

- The Abc's With Daijah B..4

- Fruit of your tree : FAMILY..5

- Circle which one fits your love style below:...11

- Crosswords that no longer cross your world 16

- Tell your body what to do: Fitness 20

- The Systems That Make Up Your Body Are:...27

- Walking forward with my L.O.A.F of bread for my soul:
  Future (Loaf=Love. Opportunity. Awareness. Forgiveness)..30

- Believing God and Yourself: FAITH..57

- Prayer:...60

- Money Mindfulness: FINANCES...61

- Activities to Try to Help Your Child(Ren) Understand Budgeting. 65

- Relationship Building Month Suggestions 132

- About the Author 136

The Abc's With Daijah B

Affirm it	:	I am..
Alarms	:	Remind yourself until it becomes a habit
Ask questions	:	Ask until you are confident in it
Better not Bitter	:	Choosing to forgive, learn and discern
Borrowed time	:	Time is not given back, use it wisely and be grateful everyday that you can wake up and smell a flower. What's your favorite flower?
Break Bondange/Borrowing	:	Limit your borrowing
Caution	:	Proceed with avoidance of problems but don't shy away from problems, welcome them.
Curiosity	:	Engage in things that spark your interest in learning
Celebrate	:	Mini-party for yourself, or whatever makes you feel good

Fruit of your tree : FAMILY

> *The planter of the seeds are sometimes unknown but the tree surely grows, knowing our mother's is knowing a piece of us. It takes time, but no rush.*
> – Daijah Barnes

Look in the mirror(mirror management work) and say:

"I love you and forgive you."

Stare at yourself and, then write down what you saw, felt, heard.

....

....

....

....

....

....

....

....

                              ....

Describe yourself happy and feeling loved. Fill the page up, draw on it if you need to. Imagine it if you've never experienced it.

Who's holding you back from that version of you?

What do you do when you're feeling happy?

....
....
....
....
....
....
....
....

Where do you go when you're happy? Who do you want to be around?

....
....
....
....
....
....
....
....

Imagine being the happiest you've ever been, so happy that you dream big or dream again.

What goal (s) would you set?

....

....

....

....

....

....

....

How would you go about accomplishing them?

....

....

....

....

....

....

....

Loaf, it's time to be that version of you. Please go and be great. Fly like a butterfly! Draw a butterfly. "Disrespect the Caterpillar, rave about the butterfly."
–Dame D.O.L.L.A

Loaf! Don't disrespect your caterpillar stage. Draw it too, haha.

Write about a time where you felt really appreciated because someone showed or told you they were grateful for you.

Circle which one fits your love style below:

Acts of Kindness/Service	:	Someone being helpful and lightening up your load. Breakfast in bed.
Receiving Gift	:	Excitement when receiving a thoughtful gift.
Word of Affirmation	:	Encouragement, Thank you's, I appreciate you.
Quality time	:	One-on-one time uninterrupted with you only (maybe family).
Physical Touch	:	Uses body language to express your love. Hug, kiss, touch.

Write a list of names of people that have supported you no matter what. That includes them going astray and coming back to be of great support. The more we express gratitude to others, the more others will express gratitude to us.

Who has tried to help you within the last 90 days? Did you accept it? Why? Or Why not? How did you feel afterwards? Why?

....
....
....
....
....
....
....
....
....
....
....

Think of 2 of those people that have supported you on your journey and you've overlooked their support, and love? Write them a thank you note. Then call them.

Person 1:

Person 2:

Think about a time where you know you were wrong for doing a specific something and you need to go back and apologize. Who are you apologizing to, and why?

....

....

....

....

....

....

....

....

How do you feel after writing that down? Are you in denial? Acceptance? Do you see yourself apologizing to this person(s)?

....

....

....

....

....

....

....

....

Do you want to become better?

....

Write 20 things that you are grateful for.

1.
2.
3.
4.
5.
6.
7.
8.
9.
10.
11.
12.
13.
14.
15.
16.
17.
18.
19.
20.

Crosswords that no longer cross your world

Resentment, trust, restless, imbalance, useless, indecisive, inconsistent, bitter, hate, guilty shame, lack, angry, fearful, stuck.

*Put a star next to any word you've felt lately.

What is the opposite of that word?

R	I	M	B	A	L	A	N	C	E	X
T	N	E	M	T	N	E	S	E	R	I
E	C	K	D	F	L	D	F	E	F	N
F	O	Y	H	X	Q	Z	S	B	S	D
U	N	T	S	U	R	T	W	T	S	E
O	S	P	S	W	L	A	C	K	E	P
B	I	T	T	E	R	H	R	K	L	E
D	S	M	S	H	A	M	E	N	E	N
A	T	S	F	A	F	L	P	S	S	D
I	E	A	S	T	U	C	K	U	U	E
J	N	D	F	E	A	R	F	U	L	N
A	T	A	A	N	G	R	Y	H	B	T

Do you have anyone in your life that you are making feel any of the feelings listed in the puzzle? Or, outside of the puzzle but you know you are making them feel a certain type of way by your actions? Why are you making them feel that way? Did you notice it before now? Do you think you should apologize with your words and actions? Will you? Be honest with yourself although sometimes honesty hurts and is embarrassing once we conquer certain characteristics we are able to be progressive in our everyday lives.

(If it doesn't apply let it fly)

Below, write the opposite of that word you put a star by in a sentence 55 times and say it in a sentence out-loud or in your head 5 times. (If you don't have any starts, choose three words)

Example: I am consistent, disciplined, balanced, rested, protected, and wise. If it doesn't apply write the opposite of one negative word that pops in your mind.

How do you feel? Take 3 minutes to write and be honest with yourself.

....
....
....
....
....
....
....
....

What do you want to do? Bucket List wise? Ex: I want to bathe in the ocean, Fly in a hot air balloon, Helicopter, Drive a mini boat and more!! Will you commit to doing one thing you like or want to do soon?

....
....
....
....
....
....
....
....

Tell your body what to do: Fitness

How do you feel about your body? What do you like? Dislike? Why?

....
....
....
....

What do you want it to look like?

....
....
....
....

What do you need in order to make this happen?

....
....
....
....

What do you have right now that you can begin to use to help you get to this look?

....

....

....

....

....

Is this look a look you truly desire or is this something you admired on someone else? Others Opinions? Insecurities?

(You owe it to yourself to be real with you, lovely loaf)

....

....

....

....

....

Look at your body right now. What do you love about your body that makes you feel amazing? (Chile, I love my thigh shape lol)

....

....

....

....

....

Look at the spot everyday for the next week and journal daily what you felt in one sentence on the lines below? (come back to this page daily)

(Ex: My curvy thighs make life multiply and acknowledge that I am one of a kind.)

1. ....

2. ....

3. ....

4. ....

5. ....

6. ....

7. ....

What does your diet look like? What are your favorite foods?

Write down what you eat for the next 24 hours.

....

....

....

....

....

Was it healthy? Was it beneficial to your body's goals whether you're losing, maintaining or gaining?

....

....

....

....

....

Look in your cabinets and fridge. What do you see? Write some here.

....

....

....

....

....

Do you see life or death? Processed or Living foods?

....
....
....
....
....

What changes could you make to balance it? Today focus on only eating raw foods or foods that are not processed. What are you going to eat?

....
....
....
....
....

How much water do you drink daily? (suggested half of your body weight so if your 200 pounds you should drink 100 ounces which is equivalent to 13 cups per day)

A. None

B. 1+ Cup

C. 3 + Cups

D. 5 + Cups

E. Not enough and I plan to change that now that I'm aware (the A in Loaf)

Choose a bedtime that will make you feel rested and ready to take on the day. Set an alarm right now and rest at that time for the next week. What time are you going to set your alarm for?

....

....

Do you know the systems that make up your body?

....

....

How old are you?

....

....

How old does your body feel?

....

....

How old does your mind feel?

....

....

Are you willing to do a 9/10 hour period of only water/prayer?

....

....

The Systems That Make Up Your Body Are:

CardioVascular	:	Consists of arteries, vins capillaries, and your heart that carries nutrients and oxygen to tissue in your body, while removing carbon dioxide and waste, and makes sure you have blood flowing correctly to all parts of your body.
Digestive	:	Break down food into small molecules in the mouth and remove through the bottom.
Endocrine	:	Releases hormones into the blood and the blood takes it to other cells in other parts of your body. It helps control your mood, development, metabolism, reproduction, and organ function.
Excretory	:	are kidneys, liver, lungs, skin which are responsible for removing waste and retaining the proper amount of nutrients, salt, and more in order to function properly
Immune	:	protection from invaders, it has the ability to identify itself and components that are not itself and respond. Three types are passive, adaptive, and innate(natural) immunity.
Integumentary	:	protects the body from dehydration and diseases, regulates/retains body fluids, temperatures, waste and consists of nails, hair, glands, and nerves.
Musculoskeletal	:	bones, muscles, tendons, ligaments, soft tissue, facilitates movement, protects internal organs, stores minerals and fat, and hematopoiesis.
Respiratory	:	Helps you breathe, pulls in oxygen from the air so your organs can work, then cleans gases from your blood like carbon dioxide consisting of pharynx, larynx, trachea, bronchi and lungs
Reproductive	:	Ovaries, fallopian tubes, uterus, cervix, vagina, eggs are produced then estrogen is secreted and fertilization occurs, then here comes the birth of a beautiful baby

The systems that were listed all need natural maintenance. Please do your research so you can treat your body well and according to its natural needs. You're on borrowed time with the body you have so do right by it so it can do right by you my lovely loaf.

Are you providing your body with what it needs? Yes or No

When you stop moving you die, which is what I've heard but how true is it exactly, absence of the soul from the body is no movement. Now my question to you is are you living or dying daily ? Living or Dying

How often do you move your body intentionally?

....

....

Listen to your favorite song today and dance to the entire song. (If possible)

Make sure you are hydrated, and stretch before doing the work (google stretches if you're unsure)

Walk/Run outside or in place for 15-20 minutes Daily

25 Squats, 25 Jumping Jacks, 25 Sit Ups, 25 leg raises, 25 lounges, 25 planks/Push Ups. (Every week add a set on week 2 do this 2x's)

Subscribe to Mirror Managements email list for future workout sessions via zoom Only available at: www.daijahb.com

Walking forward with my L.O.A.F of bread for my soul: Future (Loaf=Love. Opportunity. Awareness. Forgiveness)

What do you have in place in case of an emergency?

(Life insurance? Children Placement? Will? Savings?)

....

....

....

....

....

....

....

....

(If you don't have anything in place, no worries, begin to build beloved. We're all learning.)

What do you want your life to look like in one year? (Faith? Family? Fitness? Finances? Future?)

....

....

....

....

....

....

....

....

What do you want your life to look like in 5 years? (Faith? Family? Fitness? Finances? Future?)

....

....

....

....

....

....

....

....

Who is involved in this process? What are you going to do to get there?

Why? How does this benefit you being better?

Follow every alarm on your phone for the next two weeks.

Rest Every Saturday, and encourage your child(ren) to join, make it a challenge or offer an incentive if you can. Be sure to explain to them your why's and the importance of changing in a way that is conducive to your growth and theirs.

Each of you can say what you are thankful for and why as a starter.

Contract:

I .... am willing to do the work to change my life, so I am going to continue to assess, address, and educate myself so I am continually progressing and choosing to live.

Signature: .... Date: ....

Thank you .... (your name) for always showing up for me and never giving up on me regardless of the situation I put you in. I love you so much and forgive you for not knowing, and I'm excited to see where we are going. (Use this same format for everyone that you are thankful for, remember it is a choice for others to invest their time and energy into us.)

As you age gracefully remember that our bodies are aging, our minds, and souls should as well. Wisdom comes from experience (often assessing others' situations), reading, praying, listening to the wise elders, and others that have genuine respect and love for us. The systems that our bodies are uniquely designed with are all in alignment with God. You were made in the image of magnificence, and those systems work together for your greater good.

Motherhood is a hood that only mothers know, and can go of course it isn't easy at times but with effort every season is a breeze even through hard times mothers still choose to grind the best way they know how to. Before you were a mother you may have known many mothers but the mothers we'll write about in this section here will be your grandmother and mother.

What do you remember about your grandmother when you were younger? How did she respond when in Love or Pain? What strengths did she possess? What did you learn from her? How did she respond when someone made her upset? When she was excited? When the children weren't acting right? When challenges came up? What did you admire about her? Do you know about any of her pregnancies? If so, What? If it was in your grandma it is in your mother and you too!

If you have the luxury: Ask your mom how her pregnancy was with you. If not, record your pregnancy with your child or one of your children below. (You can ask relatives about your mom's pregnancy as well.)

....

....

....

....

....

....

....

....

....

Are there any similarities or differences in pregnancies between grandma, mom and you? Living conditions? Attitude?

....

....

....

....

....

....

....

When you are hurt by someone, what is the first emotion you express? (Ex: I always felt useless so it was my go to emotion even if someone was genuinely correcting me.)

Take a moment to think back to the first time you remember feeling your go-to emotion. (Ex: My biggest fear was feeling useless to anyone. The first time I remember feeling useless was when my mother got a new boyfriend and he pretty much took over my job of caring for my siblings and assisting with cooking and I remember me and my mom getting into a debate and she told me she didn't need me to do it anymore. Of course the load got lighter but I felt the need to be needed, and my need felt rejected. Uselessness came back when I got cheated on because it gave me a feeling of I do not need you any more, and that was the hardest thing for me to accept, even though it wasn't necessarily true.)

Do you think it is a second-hand emotion? Yes or No (Meaning you could have adopted this response from your mother while you were in the womb or from your mother or grandmother as a youth based off their responses)

What triggers that feeling or emotion? Think about a time you felt that and what happened right before you felt it.

....

....

....

....

....

....

....

....

How do you feel your mother did as a parent? Where do you feel she lacked? What strengths does she have?

....
....
....
....
....
....
....
                                        ....

Think of a time you may have seen or heard of your mom hurting. What was her first emotion? Is it similar to yours or grandma's?

....
....
....
....
....
....
....
                                        ....

What are you grateful that you learned during your childhood that you use today to keep you sane/protected?

Based on the knowledge your mother had about motherhood do you think she did her best? Why? Why not? (Think about the mothers she surrounded herself with as well)

Write your mom a thank you note. (Ex: Ma, thank you. Through your best works I learned how to survive. I also learned that sticking together is important. I thank you for doing the best that you knew. Without you there would be no me, so thank you for choosing to endure hardships and giving me life.) Make it specific to your situation with your mother.

How do you feel about giving that letter to your mom? If you're comfortable and have the luxury of calling, texting, video chatting, and you want to let her know, do so. Reminder, some of our mothers aren't ready to receive healing so it may take you to break the curse and do the work. Let the negative flow through your body like water does if that's the case. It doesn't belong to or in you for long, so do not embody painful words from anyone. To the ones not fortunate enough to have the presence, read it out loud and release it in air as if she carried the words away in acceptance.

....

....

....

....

....

....

....

....

....

** Now, Set an alarm on your phone and label it "Pray/Forgive/Heal/GetForgiveness With/for/from Ma, Mom, Mommy, Mum.."

Go look in the mirror and say ("I love you. I forgive you and thank you for always being there for me. You are amazing.) Give yourself a big hug.

What did you see? Feel? How are you feeling?

....

....

....

....

....

....

....

....

Fatherhood is important, but many of us have co-created with men who do not have healthy relationships with their fathers, or he's and was absent, So they do what they know, and that isn't excusing them of being decent human beings to us or their child(ren) but it acknowledges the error. Joy Degruy said she read somewhere that the goal was to take the strong man out of households and make the woman dependent on the system. I thought about it, I didn't do the research, but I thought about the many single women I know and hiding my stepdad's clothes back in the days and even my former partners when I entered dependency on federal programs. The man wants and desires to feel appreciated and oftentimes our strong willed unchanging, masculine energy goes against the grain. How can you do what you were never taught to do? Learn it through watching others experiences and of course your own. We're striving to be better not bitter.

Do you remember how you felt about your child's father during your pregnancy? Write it below.

How do you feel about him today? Why?

Are you hurt/hurting by his actions? Yes or No

What are you grateful he taught you?

....

....

....

....

....

....

....

....

....

Write him a thank you note. (Ex: I'm grateful that you cheated on me, because if not I'd be sitting in misery. You taught me to express righteousness and truth through your lies, and now I apply that to my life, but what if you hadn't done those things I'd probably be unhappy and stuck with a ring. I am now free to recreate my reality for which I'm grateful.)

....

....

....

....

....

....

....

....

Do you see any similarities between him and your parents? If so, What?

....

....

....

....

....

....

....

Set an alarm on your phone and label it ("pray for _____ your child's father name) remember affirming and praying for them doesn't excuse anyone from being a good human, but it merely frees you and encourages healing and forgiveness if you haven't already. Go ahead and free yourself. Praying for them causes a spiritual war and change is going to come. The more you do it the stronger you become, and the more control you have. You are much more powerful than you think. Knowing that you have no control gives you full control.

Children are created out of passion. Normally some version of love creates them. Love is defined and designed by the person(s) experiencing it. Sometimes our versions of love aren't actionary and are toxic. Every child's birth was and is unique. Let's think of them as such.

What type of relationship do you have with your child that you co-created?

Is it healthy? Abusive? Non-existent?

....
....
....
....
....
....
....
....
....

How do you feel the child you co-created with him changed your life for the better?

....
....
....
....
....
....
....
....
....

Write your child a thank you note. (Baby, I'm so grateful to have you. You show me everyday that determination, fearlessness, creative thoughts, love, and trusting God is all I need to be balanced. No-one but you could ever show me in that way and i'm so happy I get to help train you in the way you should go. I love you so much.) -Add a gift they like if you have that luxury, take a walk with them, or get creative if you decide to give them the note: Make copies of it because when the going gets rough you may need to read your own work)

Set two alarms on your phone:

1. Pray for your child/give thanks for them

2. 5-60 minutes per day with you and your child only (each child needs their own time)

   (This could definitely be a weekly thing too just plan out for it boo) For example, spend 10 minutes with your child talking and finding out their interest so you can connect on that level and begin to build a bond if you haven't already. Your child(ren) is amazing and they will be great leaders, so start them now and it doesn't matter if they're sixteen or older as long as they're willing to heal with you. The window of opportunity just reopened and you will gain patience and more Loaf (Love, Opportunity, Awareness, Forgiveness)

Record what your child (ren) does for the next 24 hours.

Did you find any wasted time? (One thing we do not get back is time so it's important to invest our time wisely) Yes or No

Can you incorporate their schedule with yours to make things easier for you? Yes or No

If so, when will you start? Date:

....

....

(Schedule 1:1 with your child so you can listen and find out more about him/her).

What's the date and time?

....

....

Believing God and Yourself: FAITH

Mirror Management Works: In the mirror say "I love you, I forgive you, and need you to survive." (Hug yourself instantly after) (Then Take 3 deep breaths)

How do you feel after saying that? Drink a big cup of water and let go of whatever came up that doesn't serve your personal development.

....

....

....

....

....

....

....

....

Write 11 "I am" affirmations (write them as if you are already the woman you want to become.)

....

....

....

....

....

....

....

....

....

....

....

Look in the mirror and say those affirmations to yourself. Did you say it like you believed it? If not, go and do it again.

....

....

....

....

....

....

....

....

Do you believe the wind provides oxygen and strength, even though you can't see it?

....

....

What would you describe God as?

....

....

....

....

....

....

....

....

....

Do you believe you were made in God's image? Yes or No

....

Prayer:

God I come to you humbly in search of guidance and a clear understanding of what's next. I want to be better but I can't do it alone, so as you sit on your throne, and I sit here alone, I ask for guidance, encouragement, a sign, support, or something better. Thank you for creating me in your image, and protecting me and my family. Amen.

Money Mindfulness: FINANCES

What type of relationship do your parent(s) have with money? Are they good at paying bills? Always evicted? Careless? Well off? None?

....
....
....
....
....
....
....
....
....

What type of relationship do you have with money? Did you grow up in a household that modeled healthy money relationships? Do your children know about budgeting? Savings? Are your habits similar to your parent(s)?

What type of relationship would you like to have with money?

....

....

....

....

....

....

....

What monthly bills do you have? (Rent, Transportation, Cellphone, Groceries)

Visit the link below for a free printable budget sheet: (https://daijahb.com/free-resources)

....

....

....

....

....

....

....

Write a list of people you owe including student loans, banks, cousins and auntys too.

Are there any excessive bills/outings that you can cut out to begin paying who you owe? What?

Are you an emotional spender? Is shopping therapeutic? Does it affect your spending habits? How? Are you passing the baton to your children? What kind of spender are you?

Activities to Try to Help Your Child(Ren) Understand Budgeting.

1. Talk with your children about cutbacks "Because of my poor choices, I owe a lot of people money and need to get out of debt, so some things have to change for a little while because my budget has.

2. Have your child go to a store and purchase $7.00 worth of food for breakfast, lunch, dinner and snacks. Do not give him/her over (amount chosen) $7.00 and allow them to think critically and become strategic with their purchase. My daughter was the winner of our $7/day meal challenge. She chose to go to family dollar and she purchased $1 Box of Maple/Brown Sugar oatmeal, $2 Pickles, $1 Frozen Broccoli, $1 Crackers, $0.80 Can of beans, $0.50 chips. (All of this is vegan, but processed. Fresh is best but it was a test.) This will give them a sense of budgets and how they work at a beginners level.

3. "No-one or thing supplies my financial gain. My God-given gifts will allow me to experience financial abundance."- Have your children repeat after you so they do not repeat the cycle of toxic money relationships.

4. Google new words that you don't know pertaining to budgeting or money handling with your child. Here's a few suggested words below to look up if you are not familiar with them. If you are familiar, broaden your horizons, Loaf.

Life insurance/ Whole life Insurance

Stocks

Assets

Liabilities

Budget Sheets/Budgets

Credit Reports

Record what you do for the next 24 hours

Did you find any wasted time? Where?

Who in your household has chores? Can you begin to assign weekly chores? Team work makes the dream work. If an area doesn't apply to you, don't fill it out.

Kitchen : ....

Livingroom : ....

Bathroom : ....

Bedroom : ....

Entrance Area : ....

Attic : ....

Basement : ....

Garage : ....

Backyard : ....

Breakfast : ....

Snack : ....

Dinner : ....

Utilize Your Resources Momma: That is what they are there for! Make it work for you and your situation. Knowing what lies within your community (Intentional Lies because some folks will hold out truth on you but it is up to you to seek, find, open doors and carry a sista with you.)

There are services like Wic(Women.Infant.Child), Snap(Food Program), Food Pantries, Certificate Programs, Incentive based programs and more. Call your local help hotline and ask questions. Keep asking questions, that's how you find out about things that serve you. See if you qualify for Affordable housing

Find programs that serve mothers only

Seek help and accept it

Instacart (Accepts Ebt: For Aldi's/Tops only for now)

Walmart delivery services (Accepts Ebt)

Amazon prime (accepts Ebt)

Museum For All

Try new delivery companies (They offer free codes to use their services) Empower is a mobile banking app (there's many apps to research) that assist with savings goals and more

www.singlemothersgrants.org

Listening Celebration Link (https://youtu.be/LFAEom4FVok)

Sit in one spot, release the tension in your arms, body and legs, you can also lay if you want to and listen.

**Find some time to celebrate yourself today. That could include but not limited to:

Praying, journaling, sipping chamomile tea, a massage, a nap, a podcast, lighting a candle, cleaning, a hot bath, but be really gentle with yourself today.*

This next section you will read quotes of healing ones that I assumed my guardian angel would have said from the sideline, or maybe just something

I needed to hear in the moment. You will also read short stories and quotes that I wrote which mean something but what they mean to you may differ. Enjoy your reading and writings.

Dear Daijah,

You are fresh out of the womb, and it's like a new moon just came and sat next to the hospital to ensure the awakening of your mother, who lay in the bed breathless and hopeless. She understood that she did not have to co-create life, but her fight to be better wouldn't let her lose her might.

Accidents happen, especially when there is no knowledge. Accidents sometimes create great change, and you are a change agent.

Dear Daijah,

You smiled for the first time and you made me smile, it lit the entire room up. I know you are divine, the womb was dark and you graced this world so wonderfully all because you chose to be you fearless. Nobody knows the fight you had in the womb, but even there you knew you were one of the chosen few. Your smile with no teeth, gumming everything let me know that everything will be okay, and not only for a day. Your bald spots let me know the spot that we are in is an incubator for love leaving you with a spot to be reminded of. Your tight hugs and extra slob made me sob, even knowing you were a chosen one, and the future fights you'd have to fight. You crawled and I was appalled. Amazed at how you rocked back and forth and sprinted forward right on your head and let me know what I was in for ahead.

Dear Daijah,

You stepped out on faith and knew you would fall, but you got back up. I watched you study your feet unbalanced because they wouldn't meet to keep you stable all to do it over and over and over until you stood upright. Holding on to the kitchen table oooo honey chile you were not stable and you sent my blood pressure to the sky! I almost felt like I could fly over there and catch you before you could hit the floor, but that just opened the door for you to soar. Your courage fuels me with faith like never before.

Dear Daijah,

You got into the pots a lot, but you weren't cooking a thing. In fact you might've taken your diaper off and put it in the pot and banged on the bottom of it after throwing around some divine intellectual quotes of "ahbathabaaataaaa". Still unstable, I wanted to cradle and protect you from everything I knew this world had to offer. Chile my blood pressure up thinking about it right now. Baby go soaring, but be vigilant about where you are flying to is all I could say at this moment to you, boo.

Dear Daijah,

Your balance is magnificent and those pull ups have a smelly scent but that doesn't stop my love for you. I am so grateful for your presence, my love, it is a present. I know you saw the cops for the first time and it scared the life outta you. I wanna hug you so tight with all of my might because that's what you need and I know no-one can see the pain you feel, but I do. It's okay to hug your baby brother for comfort, but know my steps are right in front of you.

Dear Daijah

I know you like jokes, they're your only hope. I see the pride you take in being the oldest and you wear it well. Stay out of that kitchen before you burn the well dry and the house too. I know you want to take away your mommy's pain, but baby do not go insane. That's a grown-up business and you are not that yet. Even with that little sassy mouth and ponytail, you aren't there.

Dear Daijah,

I know you miss your dad, and it makes you cry to think that he doesn't love you but I assure you baby that he is lost too and doesn't have a clue in the world of what to do. Trying to find his way in this world like everyone else, lost, hurt, abused and confused. But I don't want you to stay bruised by that my love. This is a plug of love, me sending extra love into your room tonight hug the pillow extra tight.

Dear Daijah,

I know you love your mom, and you just want to lay on her and hug her, but it's your new baby brother's time to receive care because he can't care for himself and I know it doesn't give you any ease, but if you mustered up the courage to ask she might just say yes. I don't think she'll yell at you today because it's what she needs.

Dear Daijah,

You haven't been forgotten, beloved. The man that's here didn't replace you but he's here to help. I know you don't see it like that but mothering isn't your job right now but maybe in the future, and your mom has help now. Don't feel forgotten, and or useless. She said that because you made her spirit uncomfortable. Continue to speak boldly but in your boldness be respectful to everyone including the one who risked her life for you.

Dear Daijah,

Being betrayed hurts, you wanted to test the spirit but you know what you felt, it's your divine intuition stepping up, and challenging the inner demons that it sees, this race is the race your great great great grandmothers faced.

You can get through this, let's talk about it, and confront the beast that is within that broken adult. And you can do that as a child, but don't act wild, and do it with a smile.

Dear Daijah,

You're not wrong. The decision you made was based on the knowledge you were given. Don't give up, but you oughta talk to people how you want people to talk to you beloved.

Your momma is still the one who willingly risked it all for you.

Dear Daijah,

I know you are scared and feel abandoned. Keeping it a secret wasn't the best thing, in fact getting it out sooner would've caused less turmoil but it happens, you are now ready to do what your mother did and create life.

You may not have had puberty talks, and education on sex, but this baby is going to change the rest-of your life.

Dear Daijah,

Don't cry beloved, I know you trusted him and he betrayed you especially after you sacrificed your life to bring forth his child. I know you want your mom and don't know what to do but here's a clue: go look in the mirror, and stay there. Look deep, and begin to think, but don't shrink.

Dear Daijah,

I know it happened again and again and now here comes another baby. Your mom felt this uncertainty with you and it's okay boo you'll get through this too. After her birth, apologize to your womb, and let's get in tune. It's time to make peace with your whole body.

Dear, Daijah,

Your pheromone will release healing, and many may flock, but don't go sleeping around the clock just because it is the attention you never got. Well, suga your time here is limited, so make it divine. Those souls that will come will mirror you, and when they do be grateful. Learn, grow, and glow!

Baby.

Dear Daijah,

Your desire to become new isn't unnoticeable. A gentle giant could see the light that radiates through you. Be progressive in all your ways today's a new day and you're showing it by doing things a new way. The dark can't stand your light so darkness will always take flight but be sure to assess those in your presence.

Today my footprints are here and tomorrow they may not be so it's up to me to build my community and legacy.

What does this mean to you?

....
....
....
....
....
....
....
....
....
....
....
....
....
....

When I face things that are hard I tend to feel a pain in my back, which makes me react fast. Then I'm stuck with two things to face: the stress I embodied and the message I learned.

What does this mean to you?

When I look into the mirror to manage my thoughts, sometimes a dark hawk tries to come out. Then I choose if I let her sprout. Killing the old version of me daily has become a new thing almost like a new dream. I won't stop

What does this mean to you?

I looked into my mom's eyes and I saw my great grandmother. It was like ripping a sheet off of a bed and being able to see the stains someone else left but tried to cover up.

What does this mean to you?

When I look at my daughter my eyes no longer wander. I can now look her in the face and say I love you without feeling like my heart was racing in uncomfort. Love is defined by the person who holds it. Her love showed me how to hold it close.

What does this mean to you?

The man who tugged at my heart again after I told him what he was doing caused more damage, but after mirror management work I now know he only ripped the bandaid he saw off because he wanted to heal a wound he had no natural knowledge of healing.

What does this mean to you?

My mother's fear made her jealous of my lack of fear. I had begun to live a life she had only dreamed of. Then her stab in the back to live the dream hurt someone's spleen, and that someone was me.

What does this mean to you?

I looked in the mirror again. The second time it was something within. I didn't see It clearly, but it felt unruly. I need to go back.

What does this mean to you?

The moment I noticed my daughter lied fluently I looked in the mirror and prayed that it no longer lie in my belly or be in tune with me. She was practicing to be a future me.

What does this mean to you?

I always said I attract broken people to heal them but the broken person that was being healed through them was me. I never even saw that they were a reflection of me in some way. It was like fastening my seatbelt and driving away with no rear view mirror.

What does this mean to you?

If manipulation was a drug I'd be high. It wasn't until the mirror told me that I needed to come off of the narcotic and become clean. I was a manipulative being. Today it stops with me.

What does this mean to you?

Jealousy is a trait that can be passed down to generations. When I received it and acted on it I knew each time it was something that should have been uprooted.

What does this mean to you?

Tears, and sweat taste the same but they both brought a different pain in my life to keep me sane.

What does this mean to you?

Bitterness promoted more jealousy and anger, but after a few calendar years, I sought after the real me embedded under the second hand emotions I got from everyone except me.

What does this mean to you?

Motherhood in my house wasn't sacred so I chose not to take it seriously. Now, I'm furious because I have to unlearn and relearn the purpose of a mother with a new definition: Nurture, genuine love, guidance, respect, integrity, gentleness, prayers, and peace.

What does this mean to you?

When I found out the backstabber had karma too, I decided immediately to let go and let God handle all dues owed to me. I knew for sure there would be things I experienced because I sowed seeds of genetically modified fruits, but that is my truth.

What does this mean to you?

My mom's r&b blues triggered me every time I heard a certain tune. It was all created in her womb.

What does this mean to you?

Out of money and time, now I grind. I'm back at the starting line.

What does this mean to you?

When I don't think about what others may say negatively, I'm living naturally, but when I second guess myself and listen to whoever else I'm letting them control what's within, and that's not a win, especially not knowing what they have within.

What does this mean to you?

The way I interact with people is a mere reflection of my state of mind. Whether it's natural or adaptive: it shows what is in me and not on me.

What does this mean to you?

I noticed every time I'm under pressure or stress I adapt, and then react in a way that isn't conducive to removing the old version of me. I must take a break and respond, responsibly.

What does this mean to you?

I like a pace that shows me stability, consistency, and loyalty. No disrespect to the roadrunners, but I win races at my own pace. I can't even imagine losing at my own pace.

What does this mean to you?

If I break a rule it is meant to be bent. Probably because it was made with no logical sense, but made cents.

What does this mean to you?

I love people but I love quiet too. I think it's the perfect balance but you choose your rondevu.

What does this mean to you?

Solve the problem, get the results, Interact with people who evoke experience, stabilize and ride the wave, but be true to who you are even if that means taking a pause, and evaluating your cause.

What does this mean to you?

The mirror in my first apartment scared me. I didn't even look at it to brush my teeth. I think me and her, the woman in the mirror, we had beef. Then we became vegan.

What does this mean to you?

Go look in the mirror. Stare for 11 seconds.

What do you see?

....

....

....

....

....

....
....

How do you feel?

....

....

....

....

....

....
....

When was the last time you stared in the mirror to look at yourself before today?

Is this something you could do daily to remove what no longer serves you?

The beauty in today is that it is in this moment. We get to use what we learned in the past to shape the future. What does your history say about you? What have you made a habit of loaf? What's one thing you'd like to change about your behavior that has created a pattern everyone can see?

....

....

....

....

....

....

....

Imagine healing with someone who has a similar tune? Imagine truth and pure intentions to create order in righteousness. What does that look like to you?

....

....

....

....

....

....

You've been rocking back and forth for a long time from sac water to earth's water. Riding the waves with grace and inhaling peace and exhaling chaos. What does this mean to you?

....

....

....

....

....

....

At this point clarity, completion, and replenishment are a definite sign that things are changing and for the greater good of you. What does this mean to you?

....

....

....

....

....

....

When you commit to something or someone you better believe you are about to grow through it because if it ain't one thing to grow through it's another.

What does this mean to you?

How I feel about myself shows up in the company I keep to help nurture me, and my responses.

What does this mean to you?

If I keep lying to myself, those lies are going to lie in my subconscious, and maybe become a part of my reality.

What does this mean to you?

Because I am not as confident in myself, compliments that are given to me could be used as a tool of manipulation. It all depends on the person that's constructing it.

What does this mean to you?

When I interrogate myself and ask "Why am I doing this" "Is this my choice or someone else's" I get to the root and find out whether I'm doing it for others or myself.

What does this mean to you?

If you begin to find your core values and you plant your feet/tree next to the water and budge not for non-sense your senses will be watered with peace.

What does this mean to you?

To show me your creator of life means that you've been thinking of creating life. Love and closeness with heat, sweat, a few fast heartbeats and planted feet marks the beginning of planted seeds in a womb full of plenty but only one is chosen to come forth and multiply, but if the union isn't in God's hands then that wasn't God's plan on this land. Your creation is sacred so be careful who you mate with. Not everyone is deserving of your divinity especially if you want to live infinitely and on one Accord.

What does this mean to you?

The hurt that I felt was familiar. One that you decided to drag me through again. Of course I had a choice and I chose to trust you with my mind, heart, womb, body and soul only to learn that you were just as broken as I was. Trying to discern and looking for pieces in broken pieces and lost love devouring and thriving on my weaknesses you took many attempts at battling your inner pimp. I hurted when you looked me in my eyes and lied. Put my family to the back of your fast paced race. Appointments alone, I became prone to single motherhood again, Therapist diagnosed and dismissed mental abuse by you, or should I say me, for letting things be. I knew life without you, but as I grow through this experience I'd say it was worth it. You taught me something: How I dare not to be, and even things that were admirable. Community, willingness to assist those you are entangled with and passion to help others be better, oftentimes forgetting the man in the mirror and the inner work needed to proceed with the healing, but that's not my fight. I can't say I adore fatherhood for you right now but I'm sure in the near future that'll be a crown you'll hold. I'll tip my crown to you and say thank you for losing a version of me I never knew existed, and helping nurture through pain resilience, persistence, loyalty, righteousness, charisma, and integrity. Thank you.

What does this mean to you?

Mama P baby I just knew your presence would forever be. When I thought of you, and couldn't see you, I should've contacted you but I felt out of place in the space coming forth to comfort and not knowing how to. Your strength was magnificent, encouragement 100%. Bark and bite you had all the might needed to sow seeds in every place you planted your feet. Youthful soul and face, a beautiful radiant woman of God, would throw a scripture before a shoe but believe the shoe would follow if needed. A tender hug, and smile that would make a conversation worthwhile. A smile that comforted your pain after being fed a bunch of scripture in Jesus name. I am grateful for each moment but this moment has taught me to accept, and rise boldly in the name you would always praise fearlessly. Thank you, Love you always, your past presence won't be forgotten. A love that never rottens.

What does this mean to you?

When the soul is returned to the sender and the body to dust in the flesh, we cut up a fuss even knowing a person is tired. When a person is exhausted in their works, God relieves them and allows the baton to be passed to the next in line. According to the Holy Bible story Joshua thought Moses was the one to make it all happen and when he had completed his portion of the assignment and his flesh had separated from his soul Joshua cried so bad but was told to rise up and complete the task, because Moses wasn't coming back. Completion happens in all things.

What does this mean to you?

Hurt little girl swinging in twirls because your dad isn't around and now you're grounded, but your mother loses her crown in your eyes, place the blame, and turn it into a game. Any task the momma never asks about the mask she sees, it's insane, afraid of the motions she'll have when the potion is spilled from her angry baby girl's lips. She said she ain't a jit no more, and got her momma thinking about her past what if's. Legit not forgiving herself for not being rich and taking care of her. Not only rich with dollars but knowledge of the most high God scared and confused but in tune they are gone. Call it deja vu.

What does this mean to you?

Blue, Yellow, Green, and everything in between. Beginning middle and end it's all within. Green is the completion of the two after conception and life is drained, but it all looks the same. Blue in the face, the whole race tells you to beat the baby and make it cry, but no case, because they wear a cape, white with a couple letters on it if you've had a baby, you've met them. Yellow stage If it ain't one thing to grow through, it's another praying you don't get betrayed by your mother. Pose to be the matriarchs but got a toxic arch in their backs, and we call it black culture. Sounds more like a vulture.

Family things f*** a ring, my marriage is going to come after I heal this inner being.

What does this mean to you?

Every time I open the door, I'm flooded with the mess that causes me stress. I reroute because a familiar face lives there. The space behind the door holds the pressure of logic and emotions, and when I open it, Like the glue on a family date, again, I become irate. I am studying my DISC, so I don't miss a beat about me to see about this separation anxiety.

What does this mean to you?

Relationship Building Month Suggestions

Monday-Friday Rest on Saturday

Day 1: Pick a book that you've never read and begin to read it. Today.

Day 2: Read a book to/with your children. Ask them: What they think will happen based on the title? What they learned.

Day 3: Invest in a small business (money, time, objects)

Day 4: Listen to someone with no interruptions.

Day 5: Open a door for someone/Hold the door for someone

Day 6: Write a reason you are grateful and leave it on someone's car or mail it to someone you don't know.

Day 7: Find 3 reasons to smile and smile 3 times today because of the thought

Day 8: Call a friend/family and ask them how they are doing.

(Be compassionate)

Day 9: Dance to your favorite song

Day 10: Buy yourself something nice (food, item, etc)

Day 11: Say No to something and don't feel bad about it

(No is healthy and a complete sentence, no explanation needed)

Day 12: Write 55 times a statement that you want to be

(I have a sound mind, and I'm at peace.)

Day 13: Substitute one meal with a healthier version

(Salad, Smoothie, or fast 16 hours no food 8 hours food)

Day 14:   Choose a word you want to live by and practice it today

(example confident: stand upright, make eye contact with everyone you see)

Day 15:   Cook a meal with your child(ren) one you've never tried

Day 16:   Color with your child(ren)

Day 17:   Talk about yourself to someone else: "I'm proud of myself"

Day 18:   Tell your child (ren) what you're proud of them for.."

Day 19:   Go for a walk, Breathe deeply inhale/exhale, or to a Beach

Day 20:   Watch an Inspiring Video on youtube

(https://www.youtube.com/channel/UCZG3lro4gsPjiLR9MN7niPA)

Day 21:   Listen to Acoustic soul,(https://www.youtube.com/watch?v=aQe44r9T35g&list=PLbG7KxO3W ypKpzlXzAje_Z26YCCM6shGx) write how you feel afterwards.

Day 22:   Sit for ten minutes and picture doing the things on your bucket list.

Day 23:   Take a nice hot bath, drink a cup of chamomile tea to relax.

Day 24:   Write a letter to your child about their uniqueness.

Day 25:   Give someone you don't know a compliment

Day 26:   Ask your child what he/she likes, dislikes and wants to pursue when they are older.

Day 27:   Think about your strengths and write them down.

Day 28:   What have you discovered you like?

Day 29:   Watch an exercise video

Day 30:   If you could start a business based on your strengths and passion

What would it be? What would you need? What do you have?

Day 31:   Write forgiveness/thank you notes. Guidance to Follow

I forgive you .... for .... because that experience made me a better woman. I am no longer choosing bitterness. If I had not experienced .... I would not have known that it is something that I do not like. I'm choosing and now have made my way on the other side, and happiness looks good on me, so I thank you. (You do not have to give it to anyone. Writing it, seeing, and feeling it will encourage your healing. Let love live in you happily)

Your goals are never too big! My goal is to inspire/support 100,000 women on their journey to betterment. Of course, the number looks large, but honey it ain't, and if I do this within 13-15 years It will only take me 7,700 women per year. You want to know how many per month? Haha. My goals are Macro (big) to some and that's okay, but I broke them down into Micro (Small) segments, so I feel like I am doing the work of continued service without overworking myself. Dream again. Be righteous in all that you do because you never know who is paying attention to you. Forreal. I had a person watch me for days exercising in a town I visited on a business trip, and they stopped me and gifted me, but that let me know that although I am protected, and God favored (s) me, I am aware that the enemy also has watchers. Be vigilant, and firm.

My greatest wish is that you received something from this book! I always say take what you need and leave the rest. I'm so grateful that you took your time and invested it into this book, to help ensure I reach the goal to heal collectively. I invested a lot of time away from my family and sleep to create this for you, because I know what bitterness feels like and I also know what it feels like to replace it with: Love. Opportunity (accept healing), Awareness (acknowledgement), Forgiveness= Loaf. Choose to love thickly when the opportunity arises (with boundaries) while becoming aware of who you want to be and the footprints you'd like to leave behind, and that will strengthen compassion and forgiveness. I'm grateful that we got to journey together this season. Continue to ride the waves with or without me. I believe in you. You are an inspiration to me, and as you grow through things my wish is that you breathe, take another deep breath and then proceed. Trust your body, and your mind, and your soul, and live as a lender and not a borrower, even though you're on borrowed time haha. Spend it wisely and if you're willing you can spend more time with me at: www.daijahb.com

About the Author

If you've ever crossed paths with Daijah or have spoken to her then you know just how amazing she truly is. If you can't find her in the kitchen, traveling, or teaching, be sure to check by the water. Her motherhood, leadership, and drive is astounding. To know her is to love her abundantly. Daijah has graced many stages from Ymca's to Usa Today, to the first black owned radio station in her town to Essence's black and positively golden and even BET. Daijah hasn't only dressed women for success in her former position but now dresses them for success mentally, spiritually, and emotionally. Please pray for her and her family on their journey, and stay in touch.

www.daijahb.com

www.ingramcontent.com/pod-product-compliance
Lightning Source LLC
Chambersburg PA
CBHW051212290426
44109CB00021B/2430